GW0871609

# The Holy Rosary

## by Cesare Falletti O. Cist.

*All booklets are published thanks to the generous support of the members of the Catholic Truth Society*

## CATHOLIC TRUTH SOCIETY
### PUBLISHERS TO THE HOLY SEE

# Contents

I. The Hail Mary . . . . . . . . . . . . . . . . . . . . . .3

   Why Pray to Mary? . . . . . . . . . . . . . . . . . .6

   Is Praying to Mary any Use . . . . . . . . . . . . . .7

II. The Parts of the Hail Mary . . . . . . . . . . . . . .11

   The Greeting . . . . . . . . . . . . . . . . . . . . . . .11

   Full of Grace . . . . . . . . . . . . . . . . . . . . . . .13

   The Lord is with Thee . . . . . . . . . . . . . . . . .16

   Blessed art Thou amongst Women
   and Blessed is the Fruit of thy Womb . . . . . . . . . . .19

   Jesus . . . . . . . . . . . . . . . . . . . . . . . . . . .22

   Holy Mary, Mother of God . . . . . . . . . . . . . .23

   Pray for us Sinners . . . . . . . . . . . . . . . . . . .29

   Now and at the Hour of our Death . . . . . . . . . . . . .32

# 1. The Hail Mary

The Hail Mary, after the Our Father, is the best known and best loved prayer of Christians in the West. Saying a Hail Mary is often the simplest way for us to pray together, or to pause for a moment of prayer in the presence of Our Lord. It is a way of pouring out our worries and cares to God, and availing ourselves of the maternal help of Our Lady.

Every Catholic instructed in prayer, knows the words of the Hail Mary from their earliest youth. Yet it is important and useful for us to know the history, content and theology that is expressed in those words.

I believe that the Hail Mary can be considered an important part of our culture, and a true profession of our Christian faith.

The Hail Mary is a very ancient text. The first part is a collage of biblical verses dating from the early centuries of the Church which was in use well before the tenth century. The next two centuries, the eleventh and twelfth, were a period of intense Marian devotion. The monks of that time and in particular the Cistercians dearly loved this early form of the prayer and the importance afforded it in monastic prayer life was second only to the Divine office. It was in fact a Carthusian who 'invented' the rosary, using the Hail Mary as a 'monologic'[1] prayer: a repetition of one phrase which allows us to contemplate the mysteries of Christ. The Dominicans adopted this prayer and spread and propagated it in the centuries that followed and continue to do so to this day.

The second part of the Hail Mary was composed towards the end of the fourteenth century. Its addition to the first part was ratified by the authority of the Church, in particular by Pope Pius V, in the sixteenth century. Pius was a Dominican Pope who attributed the great victory of Lepanto over the Muslim fleet to the people's praying of the rosary. The importance of this victory has been greatly played down by modern historiography,

---

[1] From the Greek *mono* (one) and *logos* (word).

4

but it was once considered to be Europe's greatest achievement in the defence of Christendom. The battle was won on the 7th October 1571, the day on which we celebrate the feast of Our Lady of the Rosary.

The first part of the Hail Mary is at the same time a prayer and a *Lectio Divina*; a prayer of praise and of contemplation. The words are exclusively biblical with the exception of the word 'Jesus' which was added later. That addition is however in perfect harmony with the scriptural text since it was the very same angel who said "and you will call him Jesus" (*Lk* 1:31). The Eastern Orthodox say: "You have given birth to the Saviour of our souls" which is equivalent to "the fruit of your womb Jesus" since the name Jesus means 'saviour'.

The tone of the second part of the Hail Mary is more one of supplication, heavily influenced by a late medieval spirituality in which death and sin were ever-present.

Today, we have inherited a very balanced prayer, which in common with many others contains a scriptural introduction and a meditation on that word of God. This meditation exposes our human frailty, and our need to entrust ourselves to God's power through the intercession of the Virgin Mary.

Among the many Marian prayers (the most ancient of which would seem to be the *Sub tuum*[2]) the Hail Mary has prevailed precisely because of its great balance and liturgical and theological exactness. There are no ambiguities in the Hail Mary. .

## Why Pray to Mary?

First of all it is necessary to correct the mistaken belief that Mary is somehow sweeter and gentler, in a certain sense 'nicer' than God. This belief is very much mistaken. No one loves us more than God, no one is more full of goodness or more tender towards us than He is.

There is no mediator between the Father and His children save the Son who has promised that we will become co-heirs with Him. Thanks to His incarnation, His death and resurrection, we can truly become God's children.

---

[2] *Sub tuum praesidium confugimus, Sancta Dei Genetrix. Nostras deprecationes ne despicias in necessitatibus, sed a periculis cunctis libera nos semper, Virgo gloriosa et benedicta. Amen.*
We fly to thy patronage, O holy Mother of God; despise not our petitions in our necessities, but deliver us always from all dangers, O glorious and blessed Virgin. Amen.

Mary cannot help but be a pale reflection of the tenderness of God. That reflection stems from her full and immaculate adherence to the will of God, and the consent she freely gave to her role in the economy of Salvation.

Because of our sins, we are inclined to hide from God. Like Adam we flee from His presence and try to hide from Him, to the point that we run away from heaven itself, from the presence of God, from the gaze of the Father. Praying to the maternal figure of Mary for help in this quest to escape would be useless. She herself would lead us out of our hiding place, back into the open, to meet God face to face, and to trust in Him. She would urge us to recognize that God is the source of all tenderness and come to know Him as both Father and Mother.

## Is Praying to Mary of Any Use?

Is Mary simply a shortcut or an easy way to avoid God's anger? Certainly not!

She is the reflection of the greatness of God and at the same time she shows us how desperately we need Him. She bears witness to the fact that it is possible for us mere creatures to communicate with the Creator. She urges us to abandon ourselves trustingly to God, to place ourselves completely within the plan of divine love, holding nothing back.

The Hail Mary contains and assembles all these aspects and teaches us how and why we should pray to Mary.

We should however, make a small digression to speak of the Communion of Saints. In the Communion of Saints we pray *with* the saints rather than *to* the saints.

We are not alone. We pray in the Church and with the Church. Our prayer is not a lonely cry in the wilderness, but an indispensable note that joins itself to the harmony of the song of the whole Church, of all humanity. We lend a voice to all creatures who praise the Lord.

The Church is a body, given life by the Holy Spirit, made up of living cells, joined one to another. Among these cells are the saints including, we hope and believe, all our dear departed brothers and sisters. It is they who work hardest for our good and who become channels for the power of the Holy Spirit to the entire body.

By God's mysterious design He raised Mary to special heights. Thanks to her unique relationship with Christ, and all the special gifts that accompanied and flowed from her motherhood of God Himself - her being conceived without sin, her assumption into heaven - and thanks to the depth of her theological and cardinal virtues, Mary has a privileged place among the communion of the Saints, and so too in our prayer.

In the Hail Mary, the purity and transparency of Our Lady become manifest; so much so that none of our prayer stays with her but all of it passes on to God. We begin by saying "Mary!", saluting her and coming close to her, and she answers "Jesus!" and leads us to Him. This is the dynamic of the first part of the Hail Mary.

Mary - Jesus: repeating this prayer often we slip into a rhythm that brings us ever closer to Jesus: just like the 'Jesus prayer' which is used so effectively by the Eastern Church.

# II. The Parts of the Hail Mary

---

## The Greeting

"Hail!" comes from the Greek word "*Xaire!*" which means "rejoice!" The same word in Hebrew was "*Shalom!*", a greeting of peace. This is not a greeting that stems from politeness, or a formula to introduce us into Mary's presence. Rather, it is a desire, a blessing which is directed towards her and comes to rest on all of the Church. It is a gesture that is completely at home in a scriptural context and in line with scriptural tradition. It is not a polite "good day" but an earnest desire, heralding, like the angel did, God's benevolent intervention.

Mary belonged to a people who lived in strong messianic hope, who depended completely on God's blessing. Peace, joy and prosperity, even in material terms, flowed from God's concern for his people. They were signs that this blessing had indeed been given, especially for a people that had long suffered from a lack of peace. God Himself is peace and joy, He is the one for whom they wait, the Messiah, the Holy Spirit who comes with gifts and fruits.

Saying "*Xaire!*", "*Shalom!*", the angel speaks an efficacious word: God is present and makes this promise real, by giving peace.

Thus when we salute Mary we say that:

- What we hope for is within her,
- What we believe in is found in her,
- What we love is God's beauty which makes Mary beautiful.

As we greet her we enter upon a new world, a divine world. We meet her and she brings us to Jesus.

When we greet her with the same words that God chose when realizing His plan for our salvation, we make an act of faith. We say "I believe" to the new world in which God's promise becomes reality. We come close to her to contemplate Christ living within her, He who brings us peace. She is the channel of grace, or to use St Bernard's image, the neck that bears Him who is our head: Christ.

Jesus, who was welcomed by Mary, comes to us, and we, like the three wise men, find Him on His Mother's lap. To reach Him we must tread the same path as Mary, so when we say "*Shalom*, Mary!" we also say "*Shalom*, Jesus!"

When we say "Hail!" it is a greeting of joy and exultation. We know that in Mary we see "a new heaven and a new earth... the Holy City, the new Jerusalem descending from heaven, from God, adorned as a bride for her bridegroom... then there will be no more mourning, nor sadness, nor weeping, nor pain." (*Ap* 21:1-2, 4)

## *Full of Grace*

The Greek word *kexaritomene* contains a wealth of meanings, and is very difficult to render in full in other languages. It means full of grace, favoured by grace, set in grace, shaped in grace, that is, in the love of God which invaded her from her conception and remains with her forever. It means full of a love that is efficacious, divinizing, sanctifying. Thanks to this word used by the angel, the dogma of the Immaculate Conception was born. For sin played no part in her story, and found no complicity in her. In Mary sin had nowhere to dwell, there was no separation, no distance between her and God; she depended completely on her creator. But her dependence did not deprive her of her freedom as a human being, as a person free to choose whom to trust, whom to love and whom to please. Mary knew whom to choose and gave herself completely, without reservation. She gave all and received all.

Her creator lived in her from the first moment of her existence, and He remains with her permanently, and she in Him.

The grace of which the Hail Mary speaks is God who gives Himself as a gift. Mary accepted this gift.

The angel does not use her name but describes what sets Mary apart, the fact that she more than anyone is "full of grace". It is this that makes her original, unique, and in this title we find everything that is Marian.

But what is grace? Grace is God who gives Himself to us. At the same time grace is the Holy Spirit which is God's gift through the Son. Grace is also the work of God which transfigures His creatures.

God gives Himself forever to Mary, and Mary is forever receptive to His gift. Mary embodies acceptance of God's grace. This means that in her, every action is a work of God and at the same time every action proceeds from the freely given human 'yes' to God's action.

How do we pray when we say: "Hail, full of grace"? The angel's words turn us to contemplative prayer, because we enter into a world which is not our own. It is the world of God's saving power, of His mercy, His beauty and His holiness. As Mary says in the *Magnificat*: "He looks on His servant in her lowliness", and in turn He looks on the lowliness of all His creatures. What is given to Mary is not without consequences for us, because we in turn will receive the same privileges. Mary is like a channel for grace, she dips into the infinite ocean and reduces it to a stream we can cope with. Her love is so great as to contain the whole of God, Mary is so small that when God floods her being, He becomes a man like us.

Contemplative prayer takes us to a place where we simply marvel at the Lord's bountiful goodness, and this leads us to conversion. But how?

## The Lord is with Thee

This is a greeting which we find scattered throughout the Bible; it is frequently used and is approximately equivalent to *shalom*. The presence of the Lord was indispensable for His people. If the Lord was with them they could achieve great things, but if He took His hand away from them they were lost. Moses knew that God had to be present among His people before they could leave for the Exodus. Boaz greeted his reapers with the same words: "the Lord be with you" (*Ruth* 2:4). Even today the Church preserves these words which are at the same time a greeting, a wish and a blessing. These words serve as the opening dialogue at Mass between the priest and the faithful. However, through the ages, tradition and translation have subtly changed the greeting. In the liturgy we use it almost as a well-wishing formula, expressing a hope that the Lord will be with you. In the Hail Mary however, the greeting is a statement of fact, an announcement, a good news. In fact the angel not only salutes Mary but brings to her the announcement (the annunciation) which had been earnestly awaited for many centuries. The fulfillment of Israel's hope was at hand; the pillar of cloud, the ark, the gift of prophecy were all signs that presaged and told of this final announcement.

In Mary all the prophecies are fulfilled and all waiting comes to an end. In her, God becomes truly present and she becomes the dwelling place of God, of the Word who became flesh in her womb and who joins each one of us to Himself. In Mary, humanity welcomes the Lord and gives Him its flesh. When we speak of divine motherhood we do not only mean that Mary gave birth to Him who is "God from God", but also that God dwelt in her for nine months, fed by her blood, forming a human body like ours, and beginning the process of our divinization. As St Irenaeus says: "God became man that we might become God."

In Mary's womb, Jesus remains God and man forever. Whenever we take Holy Communion a similar mystery occurs in us. The Word comes and remains in us, transforms us and unites our humanity with His divinity. God comes to dwell in us but it is more accurate to say that we come to dwell in God.

If the Word dwelt for nine months in the flesh of Mary, then we can say that Christ's flesh remained that of Mary, the very same flesh that now sits eternally at the right hand of the Father, risen and glorified.

We say "The Lord is with thee" and we believe that "the Word became flesh and dwelt among us" (*Jn* 1:14). The womb of Mary represents the whole of humanity; it is the place where humanity welcomes the divine Word. This is why Mary is seen as the perfect image of the Church which is the Body of Christ. She is more perfect than the temple in Jerusalem ever was. Even the Temple was only a pale shadow of the realities that were to come: the fullness of the presence of the Lord with His people.

The presence of Mary in our life *is* the presence of Jesus. St Bernard of Clairveaux says when we say "Mary" she always answers "Jesus". She does this precisely because she is never alone: the Lord is always with her.

The prophet Isaiah says that even before we pray, God says: "here I am, here I am." (*Is* 58:9) Thinking of this we can understand the mystery of the Visitation, the meeting between Mary and Elizabeth, and the deeper mystery that is the meeting between Jesus and John the Baptist. There we see the prophecies meet their fulfillment, we see man meet God. The two women hide within them the mystery of the other great meeting: the precursor meeting the messiah, the Voice meeting the Word, the angel meeting the one who sent him, he who prepares the way meeting He who is the Way.

"The Lord is with thee!" When said to Mary this becomes a joyous cry; for if the Lord is with her then He is also with us. She embodies all that we are proud of. Mary, the most beautiful of all women nevertheless remains one of us, made of our same flesh, sharer in our human weakness but united with Him who is God's strength.

## Blessed art Thou amongst Women and Blessed is the Fruit of thy Womb

These are no longer the words of the angel but the words of Elizabeth. This elderly woman spoke under the influence of the Holy Spirit, so the words she spoke are also words of God spoken to Mary and to us. We can all bear within us the divine Word, through obedient attention to the word of God, through brotherly love and through the sacraments. God in His bounty has given many ways to draw nearer to Him, to dwell in Him and to take Him to our brothers as a "fruit of our womb".

We speak to Mary using God's own words. The greatness of this prayer lies in the fact that in speaking to Mary we join our words to God's. However, the two blessings in this part of the Hail Mary (directed towards the woman and the fruit of her womb) ascend and descend. The fruit of her womb is Jesus, the son who is equal to God the Father, God from God. Every blessing that we give to God for His marvellous deeds is an act of praise that ascends to God. At the same time a grace comes from God to man which allows us to bless, to adore and love, to live and to be bringers of the peace that comes from God.

God blesses the woman, but she, the woman who represents the Church and all humanity, blesses God.

Giving birth in pain is a consequence of original sin, and still in the apocalypse the woman cries out in the pangs of childbirth, for the Church announces and brings the Saviour to the world through toil and persecution. Already in the Old Testament, God's goodness was often manifested through the birth of a child, and the greatest of these signs were given through barren women. But in Mary, God's blessing surpassed the blessings given to all the other women. The Son she bore wiped away the condemnation of the ancient fault brought about by the first woman. Here we can see the relationship between Mary and Eve which St Paul hints at. Eve, the first woman, brought about the ancient curse and gave birth to a progeny destined to work, suffer and die. Mary the new Eve brought blessings, and gave birth to the new Adam, Jesus, destined for glory - the first of a new progeny destined for blessedness. Eve, because of her pride, gave birth in pain, while Mary because of her humility gave birth in exultation.

When we say "and Blessed is the fruit of thy womb" we bless God and return His blessing.

The *Magnificat* which follows on from the meeting of these two women is the opening song of a new era, of the new earth, which mirrors the earthly paradise lost.

The serpent tricked Eve into turning her gaze away from the wonder of God's love, and to see Him as a rival, as a jealous tyrant. The serpent whetted her appetite for treacherous things; and Eve forgot her Creator and was seduced by creation. Mary however sings only of the Lord, she marvels at all His works: when he casts down the mighty, when He sends the rich away empty. In everything she sees only God's goodness, His mercy and His wisdom, His care for the weak, the poor, the lonely, the little ones. The *Magnificat* cancels out the dialogue that Eve had with the serpent and opens the gates for us to bless God.

Mary is blessed because she receives the one of whom it was said: "blessed is he who comes in the name of the Lord".

Jesus is the blessing for all His people; He is blessed because the favour of God the Father rests on Him; and He blesses because His whole life was one long blessing of the Father. In him the two blessings meet, earth and heaven unite.

## Jesus

We end the first part of the Hail Mary with the name of Jesus, thereby concluding the journey from Mary to Jesus. Mary introduces us to Him and, according to Jewish tradition, when you say a name you make that person present. In saying the name of Jesus we invoke a special protection, a union and communion with the Saviour.

The name of Jesus is a blessing, it saves and cannot be said properly without the inspiration of the Holy Spirit. To say the name of Jesus is to be showered with the oil of gladness and of mercy. To say the name of Jesus is to be forgiven and strengthened, given life, and taken into the source of life, the Holy Trinity to whose eternal communion we are invited. Jesus is the Truth and His name brings us to the truth that will set us free.

As we conclude this part of our prayer with the name of Jesus, we are filled with the sweetness of his divine presence and, bathed in His light, our wounded heart is healed.

## Holy Mary, Mother of God

With this new invocation we pass to the second part of our prayer. The content is less rigorously scriptural but nevertheless follows traditional patterns of prayer and theology.

In this second part we pass from a biblical prayer of praise, to a prayer of petition. The condition of our humanity, our frailty and weakness and our dependence on God is emphasized. Here we find certain similarities with the Our Father, although the Lord's Prayer is made up exclusively of petitions.

Petitioning God is a perfectly legitimate way of praying; Jesus himself made sure He taught us to ask. The tone of the first parts of the Hail Mary and of the Our Father is very familiar, almost intimate. We enter into the intimacy of the Son speaking to the Father or of Our Lord with Our Lady. The second parts however seem to bring to the fore the infinite distance between God and Man, a distance which is bridged by an unshakeable belief in God's mercy.

We are well used to saying: "Mother of God" but if we truly think about this title it can seem absurd. God surely cannot have a Mother, for He is eternal. Neither must we run the risk of believing in a theogony[3] like those we find in ancient mythology. We can call Mary the "Mother of God" (which in Greek is *Theotokos*, she who bore God, and in Latin *Dei Genetrix*) thanks to the definition given by the Council of Ephesus in 431 AD. A Bishop called Nestorius had begun to teach that this title was heretical. The Council, however, affirmed that Jesus Christ was true God and true man therefore that which could be said of Him as a Man could legitimately be said of the Second person of the Trinity. If Mary was the mother of Christ then she was the mother of God. Jesus who she gave birth to

---

[3] Story of the origin of the Gods.

in her simple humanity was indeed God. Hence from 431 onwards, the Church gave this title of Mary special prominence.

God is the Holy One, He lives in inaccessible light, He is the Pure One. If we can say "Mother of God" it is only because He himself wanted to become a Son of Man, our brother.

This is why the Hail Mary is not so much a devotion as a profession of faith in the Incarnation. It is always good to begin our prayer with an act of faith. Just as when we say "full of grace" we are acknowledging that grace has come to us, so when we say "Mother of God" we bear witness to our belief in the redemptive Incarnation and in our own divinization.

"Holy Mary!": she is the woman clothed with the sun, who cries out in the pangs of childbirth, the woman who received the disciples as her children at the foot of the Cross. She is the woman who having entered the glory of heaven has received a mother's mission to govern, educate and guide humanity.

She is "Mother of God" but at the same time she is also mother of humankind. Her greatness comes from her motherhood of God but all her privileges were given in order for her to help in our salvation.

This is why when we say "Mother of God" we also say "and our Mother" for in her Son we are all made one.

Every action of God in Mary was pure grace, but this should not take away the fact that Mary responded willingly to the mission she was given. She lived in perfect accord with the will of God, she played her part willingly in the plan of salvation, and this made her great.

We call her holy because she was a saintly mother. But when we acknowledge her holiness we do not make her unapproachable, rather we see that in drawing near to Mary we come closer to the Trinity.

Only God is holy, separate from all creation; yet every person is called to draw near to Him and receive His holiness, the same holiness in front of which even the Seraphim must veil their eyes.

Our thrice Holy God took on our human condition, and He did this in the womb of the Virgin Mary. She received the holiness of her son and passed it on to us as she passed on to her divine Son our human nature. In her divine motherhood we all participate in the divine nature and thus become holy.

When God became our brother He made us all sons and daughters of His mother. From the cross He said: "Woman, behold your son... behold your mother" (*Jn* 19:26-27).

Mary is therefore mother, daughter and sister of God; or as Dante wrote: "Virgin Mother, daughter of your Son".

When we say that Mary is Mother of God we profess our belief that God became man without losing his divinity, that the Word of God and the Son of Mary are one and the same.

We call her holy as a sign of admiration but we call her Mother as a sign of faith, a faith that calls us to conversion, for to learn holiness we must sit at the school of Mary.

What does it mean to be holy? To be other, to be different, to be not of this world (in Greek *hagios* means not of the world or without a world). "Since you have been raised up to be with Christ, you must look for the things that are above, where Christ is, sitting at God's right hand. Let your thoughts be on things above, not on things that are on the earth, because you have died, and now the life that you have is hidden with Christ in God." (*Col* 3:1-3) St Paul does not mean that we should be disembodied, but that in order to be holy we must be detached from this world, risen to a new life.

In what ways then, did Mary live this new life? First of all through her virginity which at the time was something unthinkable, a true break with the world around her and with the history of her people. They awaited the Messiah, and every woman longed to be His mother. Secondly she broke with her own plans: she put God's plan of salvation ahead of her own projects for her life. Finally she paid constant attention to the things of God: "as for Mary, she treasured all these things and pondered them in her heart." (*Lk* 2:19)

Despite having a heart directed to the "things above" she did not forget earthly charity, the care of her brothers, as at Cana.

As a mother, Mary is also the wise and prudent governess of the house of God; strong and responsible, she guides all of us with firmness to the glory of the Father.

## Pray for us Sinners

Thanks to her Divine motherhood, Mary has a special role of intercession for us among all the saints. Her humanity is united to that of Christ her Son, who took her flesh and blood. Therefore when the Word made flesh sits in Glory at the right hand of the Father interceding for us, she is united in a unique way to His intercession.

The intercession of Mary presents the Father with humanity as he intended it to be, according to its original blueprint, without spot or stain, in all its goodness. It is that goodness, that beauty, which makes God love humanity. As Genesis says after the creation of man: "God saw that indeed it was very good." (*Gen* 1:31)

We, however, are a fallen image of God because of our sins and impurities. We are not yet totally reconciled with God. Mary, however, shines resplendently with God's love, a love that is not turned in on itself because of sin, but that shines out for every person. "Love covers a multitude of sins" (*1 Pet* 4:8) and her love in close cooperation with the redeemer's love, covers the ocean of sins of all humanity. It covers the misery of our desolation, of our weakness and our rebellion. This role does not belong exclusively to Mary, it pertains to all the baptized, but in her we see it lived with particular intensity.

The obedience of one man, Christ the Saviour, was enough to make reparation for the disobedience of all humanity. "There where sin abounded, grace was greater still" (*Rm* 5:20). The love of one woman was enough to obtain God's mercy for all humankind, through her willingness to co-operate in the Trinity's merciful designs.

The Hail Mary is a prayer for us sinners. In this there are echoes of the 'Jesus Prayer' so beloved by the Eastern Churches.

When we say that we are sinners, we admit the necessity and urgency of Mary's intercession. Sin is the seed of death, a death which comes through slow suffocation. As it says in the psalms "Save me O God, for the waters have risen to my neck" (*Ps* 6:2); death swallows us up. If the Lord does not help us we are lost, there is no hope for us.

If we remain in our self-sufficiency, in our illusion of safety, then prayers of supplication like the Hail Mary seem useless and empty. We can end up thinking that prayer is a luxury that we can do without. However, if we become conscious of our sins then prayer becomes a necessity. When the boat was sinking, the disciples had no hesitation in waking the sleeping Jesus.

In the Hail Mary we ask Mary to join with us in our cry for mercy. We ask her to cry to God in our stead, for we have lost our voices, suffocated and paralysed by so many sins.

So I cry "Pray for me!" because I cannot save myself but you can obtain for me Christ's gaze of mercy. For Jesus listened to the appeal of the Syro-Phoenecian woman in the Gospel, and turned his eyes of mercy towards her dying daughter. (*Mk* 7:24-30)

I need the help of others and especially of Mary, the Mother of God and my Mother.

When we speak of sin, it is important not to think exclusively of immoral acts, and to get bogged down in feelings of guilt. Sin is also the distance that exists between the plan of God and our actual situation. It is not being a son of God like Jesus, not showing the same gaze of love to the Father that the Son shows. From the moment in which Adam hid from God, man stopped being the creature that was indeed "very good", the creature that the Trinity looked at and loved, seeing its own image. Only Mary, conceived without sin, could return man to that original image, the image of innocence.

## *Now and at the Hour of our Death*
This line of the prayer stems from thirteenth and fourteenth-century spirituality. It was a time in which the Black Death, frequent invasions and wars gave people a strong sense of the precariousness of life.

In the Hail Mary we say "now", *immediately*. We highlight the urgency of our prayer. Often we say: "pray for me" and it can be little more than a vague platitude. But if we say "pray for me now", the seriousness of our request becomes apparent.

In addition to the immediacy of our request, this line also speaks of its duration. Mary accompanies us throughout our life. Her motherly presence is always with us, and thanks to her Assumption she is also always with God, standing before His benevolent and glorious countenance. She sees the face of God and then looks at us, receiving His glory and passing it on.

We invoke Mary so that she can be present now and in every moment of our life. "Now" is not only a moment in time, it is the unchanging essence that makes up our deepest self. That part of us which, buffeted by the ups and downs of our life, the physical and psychological highs and lows, the joys and sadnesses, work and rest, nevertheless remains unchanged. The faithfulness of Mary accompanies us steadily, as the minutes slip away, towards the saving presence of Jesus, the Alpha and the Omega, He who was, who is and who is to come (cf. *Ap* 1:8), the beginning and the end, our Redeemer.

Mary is present in our lives as she was in the life of Jesus: silent and discreet, vigilant and co-operative. For this we say, "now and at the hour", almost as though these were one and the same moment. For us believers "now" is "the hour", for we live continuously passing from this world to the next in an eternal Easter.

Let us remember the presence of Mary in the life of Jesus: at His birth Mary represents the "hour" in which the mystery hidden from eternity in God comes to its silent completion. In Mary, God makes His spousal love for His people incarnate: "the two shall become one flesh" (*Gen* 2:25 quoted in *Mt* 19:5). Mary welcomes God in obedience (cf. *Lk* 1:38) and guards the mystery within her, "pondering it in her heart" (*Lk* 2:19) as if kneading the Bread that will be broken to save and unite the world.

At the Feast of Cana, it is Mary who brings about Jesus' "hour". She gently pushes Jesus to intervene on behalf of humanity (the bride and groom). The mother puts the Son in motion towards His Passion and Resurrection. The wine of the wedding prefigures His Blood, poured out to transform mourning (symbolized by the lack of wine) into joy (symbolized by plentiful wine which is the cause of joy) at the wedding of God to humanity. "For me you have changed my mourning into dancing, you removed my sackcloth and clothed me with joy." (*Ps* 29:12)

The next "hour" is the hour of the Cross, the hour of the death of Jesus. His mother was present even at this hour. Alone at the foot of the Cross she represents the Church collecting His saving blood in a cup. She offers the wine to all humanity knowing that this draught will bring back "rejoicing and gladness" (*Ps* 50:10) and that man will know the "joy of God's help" (*Ps* 50:14).

Thus when we say "and at the hour of our death" the parallels with the Gospels are very strong. This line of our prayer contains a strong sense of the passage of time: something that can cause us anxiety, especially in the latter stages of our life. We cannot make time stand still nor can we recapture it. Through the years we can count on the soothing presence of Our Lady, on one who can truly give peace and serenity.

We call upon Mary who is already in heaven in all her humanity. Our finite human bodies become infinite as we see her in Heaven, and our journey on Earth opens out to eternal life. This is why we add "and at the hour of our death".

With these words we acknowledge our weaknesses, our limitations, we accept that we are mortal, that we are not eternal or omnipotent: we accept that we are not God.

We fear the hour of our death for many reasons.

Above all we fear the suffering that may accompany that moment. We fear the physical or mental suffering that may occur as our bodies deteriorate. We fear the emotional suffering of leaving our loved ones and our cherished possessions behind. Above all, even in the most peaceful of deaths, we fear what we regard as unknown, unnatural, and even violent. Faith can help us but does not take away the apprehension, the fear or even the involuntary rebellion our being feels when faced with death. Jesus Himself displayed sadness and anxiety at the hour of His death.

However, we must not forget that beyond death there is judgement. The judge is our Saviour and should not be feared. For us to be saved there is no need to think that we will go to hell. We can live in the sincere hope that the wavering flame of our love for God will continue to burn before His love and mercy. It is certain that God wants us to be saved and he acts accordingly.

Judgement is not simply concerned with heaven and hell. God's judgement is a light that shines on our life and shows it to us 'naked' for what it is, something we always try to avoid seeing. In the moment when we stand exposed before God, will we be able to accept His unconditional love, or will we fear our nakedness?

The final judgement will force us to speak out, to finally say "yes" to God. The question is, which God will we be expecting? The generous Lord for whom we have worked hard and whose talents we have invested wisely; or the demanding master whom we fear, because He reaps where He has not sown and whose return we await with apprehension? Is He the Master whom we waited for, diligently working together with our fellow-servants even when He delayed in coming? Or did we take advantage of His absence to live in idleness, exploiting and mistreating our fellow-servants, ignoring the fact that anything we have comes from Him?

When we meet the judge face to face we will see ourselves divested of all masks and disguises. It will not be an easy moment, so we say: "pray for us now and at the hour of our death". Will we have enough faith to confront that moment of change? If Mary is with us we can face that moment with greater courage and hope.

We must not forget, however, that death is also the moment in which we will meet the 'Beloved' - the one we have sought and loved all our lives. It will be a moment of joy as we cross the divide that should never have come into existence. St Paul says "in this present state, it is true, we groan as we wait with longing to put on our heavenly home over the other; we should like to be found wearing clothes and not without them. Yes, we groan and find it a burden being still in this tent, not that we want to strip it off, but to put the second garment over it and to have what must die taken up into life. This is the purpose for which God has made us, and he has given us the pledge of the Spirit." (2 *Cor* 5:2-5)

In St Paul we see great realism at the heart of enthusiastic faith.

"Now and at the hour of our death": in this prayer is encapsulated the whole meaning of our earthly journey. We do not look back to the past with nostalgia for "I forget the past and I strain ahead for what is still to come; I am racing for the finish, for the prize to which God calls us upwards to receive in Christ Jesus". (*Phil* 3:13-14) Our hope makes us jump for joy because every time we recite this prayer the distance between "now" and the "hour of our death" decreases and we get a little closer to our final destination. If Mary is with us, what our eyes do not see will be shown to us. The heavenly banquet will throw open its doors and invite us to enter.

The passage of time can scare us even if we remember that Jesus reassures us: "I am with you until the end of time". Prayer to Mary, the first to be saved, the first one risen from the dead with Christ, with a glorified soul and glorified mortal body, shows us what lies beyond our fear: the fulfillment of the promises of Christ.

With this last line of the Hail Mary we do not so much remind ourselves of the finite nature of our life as of its eternity.

To her we entrust the journey of the Church which runs through the passing centuries to meet the bridegroom. In His eternal embrace the Church will find her fulfillment. And with her all of humanity.

*Amen*